THE POET'S GUIDE
TO THE GALAXY

THE POET'S GUIDE TO THE GALAXY

Part 1

TRACEY LINGWOOD

Copyright © 2022 Tracey Lingwood

All rights reserved. No part of this publication may be reproduced, stored in a retrieval system, or transmitted in any form or by means, electronic, mechanical, photocopying, recording or otherwise, without the prior consent of the copyright owner

I dedicate this book in the loving Memory of Thomas Matthew Collins 'Tom'

TABLE OF CONTENTS

Acknowledgments · ix
Prologue · xi

For Tom.....you were Man United · 1
Mother's guide to the Galaxy · 2
Redwood Grove · 4
Yellow · 5
Three Rooms · 6
Golden nuggets - A celebration of achievement & Inspiration · · · · · · · 8
Just in case - a celebration of the joy of love · · · · · · · · · · · · · · · · · 9
It cuts like a knife - there is no time limit on grief - for my mum Hazel · · · 10
My Love · 11
The Domino Effect · 12
Three heads are better than one · 13
Simply one of a kind · 14
Love thy neighbour · 15
Fruits of their labour · 16
...Just say NO · 17
Kings and Queens · 18
Bipolar Opposites · 19
Mrs Bell · 21
Little Miss Sunshine · 23
A river runs through it · 24

250,000 · 26
Scented dreams ·27
SMART· ·28
Sri Lanka ·29
Well I wasn't expecting that · · · · · · · · · · · · · · · · · · 31
I met her last year - Katie O'Pray· · · · · · · · · · · · · · ·32

ACKNOWLEDGMENTS

First and foremost I would like to thank my two children Lauren and Daniel. Every single day, you keep my soul wrapped in the most precious blanket of pride, resilience and above all love. From the words of my friend Jackie – I would give you the skin off my back.

To my husband Andy – aka -Dusty. Your artistic prowess has always been a source of encouragement, and creativity - my muse.

Last but not least I would like to acknowledge the exceptional work and constant inspiration to many - Daniel Wilsher. In the face of adversity - his tireless work dedicated to our future generation, and adults alike is priceless!

Into the dark went he, he shone his light so bright - over so many. They could see – touch and feel again, with guided hope and consolation.

A brighter future for them lay ahead

PROLOGUE

'The poets guide to the Galaxy' is a collection of poetry, that celebrates our humanistic feelings, where we reside under the same sky – from every corner of the globe and back again.

Tracey Lingwood

FOR TOM.....YOU WERE MAN UNITED

I will always love you
reverberated around the Vale walls
Family friends gathering
For you they stood tall

Standing room only
the golfer's in their shirts
caught the true essence
a life story did unfold
spoken so eloquently by Derek
of Tom's dashing story

The sun shone and sadly smiled
with utter unique glory

Gone are those too soon
who touch us with their grace
but we will hold them close
as the memories we hold in place

The Boxerbeat will keep playing
as Tom's legacy lives on
It's all about
the mark we make
the oh so written song

Dedicated to Tom

MOTHER'S GUIDE TO THE GALAXY

One pound 14 ounces
You are a survivor a fighter
a creator - my hit maker
You deserve those beautiful curves
that beautiful heart
your mind oh so smart
from the start
you captured my heart

I close my eyes
you never cease to amaze me
I may be your creator
but you are my saviour

You deserve like no other
beautiful mother
to be treated with such
kind love and gentle grace
someone who looks deep
into your beautiful eyes
holds your hand
walking through the rain
a desert a plain - life's rocky terrain
You deserve someone
you can put the world
to rights with
just love to guide
each other with

Above all and beyond
you deserve you
undeniably just you
for now
Your heart is also your soul
your solace your home
your voice your choice

For Lauren

REDWOOD GROVE

Kindness comes in all
shapes and sizes
colours creeds ages - and guises

Kindness for Redwood
limitless bags
again united together
they stood
collective expanded neighbourhood
shared in the grief
came together cemented belief

Human kindness
in all its glory
the town of Bedford
It's unique
own story

YELLOW

First and foremost
mentor creator
lyrical instigator
A woman of substance
nurturer of the human condition

You made the world yellow
You made me feel
10ft tall
when I felt
vulnerable
and incredibly small
Sitting on the bench
A blanket on our laps
our precious laughter – and chats

Your family did you so proud that day
family photographs friends gathered
to remember
to share cherished memories
of the lives that you touched
with such natural ease and grace
I miss your face your voice
until we meet again

For Chris

THREE ROOMS

Your once twice three times a lady
so the song goes

Three Rooms
Is delectable
Interior in sync
Moghul Cuisine
like no other before
beautiful surroundings
as you walk through the door
Ambience fit for royalty
for that I am sure

Now let's mention the dishes
Elegant
delicate sumptuous
tantalising
taste

You could be in India
If you close your eyes
The waiters are pristine - crisp - so smart

Has to be a popadom - golden chutney - to start
Prawn on puree - sauce like a silk purse
Succulent Chicken Biryani sang to my soul

A Peshwari Naan for Aladdin - a magic carpet ride
as he floats above the ever turning tide

So if you're a local
or a visitor to our town
proofs in the pudding
walk through that door
you'll experience something else
of that I'm sure

Dedication The Three Rooms

GOLDEN NUGGETS - A CELEBRATION OF ACHIEVEMENT & INSPIRATION

Not hiding under a bushel
immensely brave and strong
poetic advice to the young
and adults alike
nuggets of wisdom
certainly not contrite

His inner gold
casts a vast blanket
against the odds
that were undeniably tragic

This he turns into sunlight
as we all need to do
he does it so skilfully
for me and for you

Damaged goods
he most certainly stands tall
with giddy heights
sometimes a fall
He shines his light
on the darkness
with unique clips of such wisdom
golden nuggets
straight into your soul
his only goal

JUST IN CASE - A CELEBRATION OF THE JOY OF LOVE

Just in case
my eyes do not open
just in case that last chance
just in case that last glance

I will tell you I love you
there is no one above you
My last wish
is sealed with a kiss
for today not tomorrow
my life would be hollow

So I will tell you now
no matter how
I won't sacrifice this chance
my utter last stance

In a blink of an eye
you won't ask why
for I told you today
our love will replay
in my heart you will always stay

IT CUTS LIKE A KNIFE - THERE IS NO TIME LIMIT ON GRIEF - FOR MY MUM HAZEL

Grief can creep up on you
with a tight vice like grip
it can pull the rug from under you
when you least expect it hits

That smell drifting up your nose
potent perfume memories
transport you back in time
when you held that loved one close
wouldn't it be oh so sublime to hear your voice
once again alas there is no choice

That song that cuts so deep
as it resonates through your blood
for that special someone
who was so deeply dearly loved

The one that made you laugh
and quite equally made you cry
we can all ask the question
oh why oh why oh why

So when I close my eyes at night
I can picture your unique face
I know you are surrounding me
With your soul
your love your grace

MY LOVE

Oh how I have missed
your beauty
your majestic calm
and your storm
The shadows upon
the surface of your majesty
reflects the mood
of this day
it has been an age of wait
and anticipation

The sound of your voice
rippling through my senses
restoring my inner strength
no other can wash
through my soul
so intensely as you
Your scent purifies me
I am in awe of you
and your powers that be
my lover my solace
my faithful friend the sea

Dedication Hunstanton

THE DOMINO EFFECT

Instead of all fall down
they all stood up
they learnt to empty
their cup

They talked and shared
inspired one another
no longer keeping it undercover
Connections friends were made
they were joyous elated
no longer adrift
no longer afraid
"who am I?" she asked
to another her words made sense
the domino effect
but in reverse
a passionate verse

Dedicated to Bedfordshire & Luton Recovery College

THREE HEADS ARE BETTER THAN ONE

They say two heads are better than one
before making a decision
It must be done
friends for life

As the two swam through the ripples
with the sun kissing the pool
with the sound of water crashing swishing
with ripples of laughter
from the fellow swimmers young and old
shapes and sizes
Sun cream applied like protective armour
They mulled over their present and future plans
They mulled over their creative pursuits
They mulled over which path to take their growing roots
They mulled over under the blue panoramic sky

The evening came and another head appeared
the darkness fell and the stars shone brightly
and stared at me with a knowing look
The stars and I agreed together with a knowing wink
three heads are better than one
when one needs advice on life
someone else's point of view
to create a clearer picture for me
and certainly for you

Dedicated to Cas and David

SIMPLY ONE OF A KIND

One of a kind not simply put
from their writing of their
two unique books
Not just one of a kind
many things she has done
the list is endless

She gets vital projects underway
for the community
her passion her main stay

One of a kind so many roles and goals
she brings people together
collaboration indeed
many accomplishments
shout from her soul
united front her only goal

One of a kind
she sows a seed in her community
in her they believe as she does them
women young and old - children and men

Dedication Dee Bailey

LOVE THY NEIGHBOUR

I know she's there if I need her
for one of our little chats
her beaming smile lifts me
when I'm feeling crap
She makes the Sun shine brighter
and catches the rain in my heart
before it has time to drown me
I loved her from the start

Some people just radiate kindness
Some people just make you feel tall
when you're feeling sad or vulnerable
or your backs against the wall

Butterflies surround her
when she is missing her beloved nan
You are also a beautiful Butterfly Susannah
You flutter around spreading your fairy dust
With your beautiful wings
Your presence is a must

Dedication Susannah

FRUITS OF THEIR LABOUR

Converse rehearse
a chapter a verse
a quest we invest
in our communities
to bear fruits
for our labours
our saviours
so spread the good word
don't utter be heard
Healing is believing
Insightful
delightful
Bedford kindness for one
no job can't be done
They are prolific In support
they hold the fought
their chariot stands by
when there is need from a cry
they dust themselves down
wearing their valant crowns
They shine upon in droves
through the rain drops and cold
then the sun cheers them on
until their day is done

Dedication to Bedford Kindness

..JUST SAY NO

I know you want to
It's written all over your face
Say NO go on
Your cup is full
You are at your limit
Say no, win it, own it

As my friend Chris said to my friend Charlie
"sit on your hands, you don't have to volunteer
for everything"
alas this is easier said than done
however it must be done sometimes

But you must ! self-preservation
or your beautiful cup will overflow
and your weariness will creep up on you
life the grim reaper
fatigue burn out don't do it
empty that cup

just believe
Just say NO
Just say NO
It's ok
give it a go
NO will smile at you
and thankyou from the bottom of his heart

KINGS AND QUEENS

Now I've worked with a lot of teams
in general practice
and all uniquely different so true
but this one was quite exceptional
and I'll lay it out bare
so it's undeniably crystal clear
as they are rare

No matter how difficult or challenging a day
you can hear their laughter in sink
it bounces of the practice walls
they pick each other up
if one of them should fall
No matter what is needed
their work family group chat is on hand
it's their unbreakable friends lifeline
united stance command

As I say goodbye to them
as I start my next creative chapter
I wish them all the very best
most certainly I'll miss their rapture
Adios goodbye au revoir
Arrivederci

Dedication King St Surgery

BIPOLAR OPPOSITES

Back in 2019 at the age of 49, I was diagnosed with Bipolar 2 Disorder.

Working in the NHS at the time when Covid hit, I didn't have the time to research much and digest my diagnosis but to my relief I realised - after many, many, years, I wasn't going mad after all. It was like someone had switched a light on and it suddenly all made sense!

Living with Bipolar can be an exhilarating experience with masses of energy moreover incredible feelings of motivation ,and drive. At these times you can feel so full of creative energy, it just flows – like being on a super charged rocket, at a rip roaring, rapid rate – the sunny side, productivity at it's best. As buzz lightyear said 'to infinity and beyond.

The best way I can describe bipolar in simple terms-it's like a motorway. Firstly, the hard shoulder, you're in a very dark place indeed, barely, functioning. Secondly, the slow lane, functioning on a low level. Middle lane, well you can guess 'ticking over nicely' in 'control' as you listen to the dulcit tones of Barry White and the ever healing Coldplay.

Now – the polar opposite, as I touched on earlier ,when you end up in the fast lane (for me, usually from stressful situations) This is where the real danger lies – rapid thoughts, fast decisions, all equalling to possible disaster! - you can get the picture. Now this is what I call 'the dark destructive' side of bipolar disorder . The fall-out from this can be catastrophic to those around you, especially family and friends.

'We cannot change our past – we are in our present and our future'
Thankfully , over the last year I have been able to do extensive research into the disorder, and my best advice from personal experience, to anyone, would be to do you're research because knowledge certainly is power – the tools to stay in that middle lane.

If I can suggest one book out of all those out there on Bipolar Disorder and there are many, I recommend **Kay Jamieson** and her very insightful (life changing) **The Unquiet Mind**. She is a renowned psychiatrist and fellow sufferer of Bipolar Disorder. The read is worth it's weight in gold.

Lastly, but certainly not least – I dedicate this part of the book to Jenny Doe a true inspiration to me. Jenny has had a long career as a Psychologist for CAMHS. Jenny sent me a message one day **'I also think poetry saves lives'** This reminded me of a song **'Last night a Dj saved my life'** She also messaged recently about this new book…… **'Power to your pen'** - so let's get back to poetry.

MRS BELL

Teacher creator literacy progress maker
Mother daughter sister & dear friend
We miss you
What we shared at Lakeview School
will stay with me forever
a warm place in my heart

Year 6
One of the best years in my teaching assistant profession
Miss Peacock's class
like the bird she was beautiful
with a lovely warm smile
and a gentle way about her
Being her assistant was an absolute pleasure
always kind as we worked in sync - as teacher's and teaching assistants do

The beauty of that year supporting Miss Peacock was that this year 6, was a new in-take with around 18 children

12 less than was the norm for a class, this meant we could give so much more

Preparing children for their SATS can be a stressful undertaking for the children and staff, but we did it with determination, resilience and pride

Furthermore. Teaching children emotional intelligence is a vital part of the role, as any adult in a school will tell you – yes academic prowess is fundamental in a child's future, but so is the ability to thrive in peer groups to grow happy, positive, healthy relationships with others

I know that Miss Peacock and I instilled that in the children too

We worked hard - we worked together

These are the highlights
Miss Peacock and I pretending to drive a car to help the children learn to give directions - they laughed, they learnt
When it was easter and I was given easter eggs by staff. I placed them on my chair by my little desk
The children made me laugh as they wanted them
When they were outside at break I took the eggs out of the boxes and hid them
Discretely placing the empty boxes back on the chair
When they came back from break I promptly sat on the empty boxes
The horror on their face, that I'd squashed my eggs was priceless
as was their laughter afterwards
when I got the eggs out of the cupboard I'd hidden them in
It's all about relationships we build with each other from the get go
The last day tears that were shed, after their leaving assembly, of which they sang their own version of Take That's 'Never Forget'
To me that signified what the impact all staff in schools have on our young peoples,1 lives and futures

LITTLE MISS SUNSHINE

Little Miss Sunshine shines her rays
across our grey little car park
she swirls around on her little bike
chatting away to me when we meet
In the street

Little Miss Sunshine loves unicorns
and pretty things
that all little girls dream of
she loves her sparkles and dresses
pastel shades her brown tresses

Little Miss Sunshine has a cheeky smile
this cheeky smile goes on for miles
as far as the eye can sea............
she brightens the day for me

For our little Butterfly - Amelie

A RIVER RUNS THROUGH IT

The people of Bedford and our communities
deserve this day as they have waited so long

The river festival triumphs through its dancing
all styles from Sri Lanka to Bollywood
Satchi danced moving her arms so gracefully
like the neck of a swan – so serene and fluid
The river runs through it as the singers sing
a true river festival fir for a King

The river runs through it
Delectable smells of delicacies that are mischievous
as they envelope your sense of smell – surely heaven not hell
Sizzling, steaming, whistle top screaming, sung the chorus
Sunny Turmeric, arrays of spices - heady height-ness

Succulence sauciness faultless flawless
Crunch munch lunch brunch, pink clouds of candyfloss
Cooking onions chatting, until the dreaded scoop tips them
Into the, oh so lonely, hot dog roll
He had been sat there waiting patiently
like a canoe on rippling crystal clear water
Mustard or Ketchup? sang the bottles - competitive little chaps

The river runs through it
As they clink there glasses together over a
Pimms some Gins a beer no fear it's here
Friends family communities
united together on this glorious two day fiesta

Businesses celebrate home grown talent
In rapturous applause - Goodacres
where a home is not just a home
It's a dwelling a nest you invest

The river runs through it
Clarity now
Charity
A vision of what Bedford is proud of
volunteers from all sectors
causes true sources leaflets advice
come join us the pamphlets say
come visit or stay
Spread the word like the Hovis boy
running by the river - not down the street
charity meet and greet

The river runs through it
as the boats drift along
Beautiful Bedford
alive with a heart beating so loud
above their bird song

250,000

Guestimate – estimate
They came they saw they conquered
In their droves to our town
yes our town our crowning glory

The fire engines sat there
Red in the summer sun
our heroes
who fight infernos
for who knows
like the hose pipe
what's around the corner

The army trucks
Spoke of safety - proudly over looking
Our GREAT river Ouse
For the children and adults alike to peruse

SCENTED DREAMS

Her bespoke stall
full of all
beautiful things
from the ribbons wrapped around
her legs - she is unique - so creative
She gives - 'Not on the High St' a run for their money
Inspired, dragon fired

www.scented **dreams.co.uk**

SMART

They are smart I knew that
From the start
James talked passionately
about this cause open door
raise the roof not aloof
Homelessness – helping people to help themselves
Tools of the trade inspiration made
They get by with a little help from SMART friends

www.smartcjs.org.uk

SRI LANKA

Now let's put this on the map
From the beautiful wildlife……
The tigers eyes piercing – such grace
as he lays on a rock he is easy to spot
Aqua coloured peacocks with feathers for hats
Majestic elephants – animal kingdom cats

Crystal clear waters the stunning views
A warm welcome is waiting for you
A place for solace – or to inspire you
fire you invigorate, enlighten you
Adventure awaits - only you can create…….

Rock climbing and trekking
It's all beckoning
memories to make
Polo and golf on a carpet so green
It looks so luscious – oh - so serene

Take a step off the plane
to see what I mean
Medicinal healing so tranquil awaits
only you, can open the gates

Festival of lights -ready to inspire
ready to set your world on fire - catapult you higher
Vibrant colours like a peacock fan
whether you're a boy or a man

Steeped in culture the art is laid bare
Close your eyes just imagine, you're already there……………..

Dedicated to Dr Roshan Jayalath and the people of Sri Lanka

WELL I WASN'T EXPECTING THAT

Well I wasn't expecting that
Or was I…..
For awhile I could sense something
something special
something rewarding
something with soul
spiritual guidance
something heart changing
book making
celebrating

I just sensed it
It's hard to explain
an epiphany
the Robin, she whispered to me gently
stroked my face with her wing
Acacia Blue – the Butterfly
danced in unison
as we all celebrated together
triumphant this day had arrived

For the people of Sri Lanka & in loving memory

I MET HER LAST YEAR - KATIE O'PRAY

I met her last year – Katie O'Pray
Poet, daughter, sister, friend
lyrical creator, what she has to say
is genius infectious insightful
utterly delightful

Passion in her pen
For the spoken word she celebrates
Creates
fine pieces of art
Bespoke leaving her mark

This world shines brighter
for her words so powerful
challenging so inspiring
firring on all cylinders
words from her truth
most of all inspiring our youth

Dedication Katie O'Pray

This book has been such an intense and pleasurable experience to write.

Celebrating humanity, kindness, and all the worlds beautiful colours, in our communities - far and wide.

The sequel, to 'The poet's guide to the Galaxy' is going to be so very special – Rudi will open the book, and then our young people will take over. I already predict - it will be my best collection so far......

Much love

Tracey

Printed in Great Britain
by Amazon